Why
Willows
Weep

Why Willows Weep

Contemporary Tales from the Woods

Edited by Tracy Chevalier
Illustrated by Leanne Shapton

Indie**Books**

Why Willows Weep:
Contemporary Tales from the Woods

Edited by Tracy Chevalier
Illustrated by Leanne Shapton
© Woodland Trust 2011

This edition © IndieBooks Ltd 2016

ISBN: 978-1-908041-32-6

IndieBooks Limited
4 Staple Inn, London WC1V 7QH
indiebooks.co.uk

Printed in the United Kingdom by
CPI Antony Rowe, Durham, DH1 1TW

Printed on FSC-certified paper with
processes certified to ISO14001

1 3 5 7 9 8 6 4 2

Contents

Foreword

Trees and writers share a long and intimate history. Ever since Gutenberg's printing press, books have been made primarily on paper derived from wood. Writers owe trees a great debt for enabling them to communicate so elegantly with the world.

To show their appreciation, some of the UK's favourite writers have headed into the woods for inspiration. *Why Willows Weep* is the result: nineteen writers, nineteen UK native trees, nineteen grown-up fables, written especially for this collection and illustrated by our twentieth contributor, the author and artist Leanne Shapton.

Every book sold supports the work of the Woodland Trust, the UK's leading woodland conservation charity. As well as caring directly for more than a thousand woods across England, Scotland, Wales and Northern Ireland, the Trust also works with landowners and local communities to plant new woods and protect ancient woodland. Its vision is to double native woodland cover in the next forty years.

For their talent and generosity, we would like to thank all of the authors, as well as Jonathan Drori, Josephine Greywoode, James Humphreys and Emily Wood.

We hope you enjoy these tales. And we hope too that you will spread the word: UK trees need our help. They are not only essential to our well-being, but to books and writing too.

Happy reading—
Tracy Chevalier and Simon Prosser

Why the Ash Has Black Buds
William Fiennes

The trees have always had some idea of what happens to them when they die. In forests they saw their neighbours toppled by wind or age and rot into earth, and their roots sent up descriptions of peat and coal in vast beds and seams. Later, when humans came along, trees saw the stockades, the carts pulled by horses, the chairs and tables set out in gardens, and quickly put two and two together. Trees growing beside rivers saw themselves in the hulls and masts of boats, and trees in orchards understood that the ladders propped against them had once been trees, and when men approached with axes to fell them, the trees recognised the handles.

Trees often wondered what their particular fate might be. Would they subside into the long sleep of coal, or blaze for an hour in a cottage grate, or find themselves reconfigured as handle, hurdle, post, shaft, stake, joist, beam – or something more elaborate and rare: an abacus, a chess piece, a harpsichord? And out of these dreams a rumour moved among the trees of the world like a wind, not quite understood at first, it was so strange – a rumour that when they died, instead of being burned, planed, planked, shimmed, sharpened, many trees would be pulped. This was an entirely new idea to trees, whose self-image was all to do with trunk, sturdiness, backbone, form. But trees are good at getting the hang of things, and soon they understood that from pulp would come the white leaves humans called *paper*, and that these leaves would be bound into books, and after a short season of anxiety in which conifers shed uncharacteristic quantities of needles, the trees came to terms with this new possibility in the range of their afterlives.

Yes, the trees recognised themselves in paper, in books, just as they recognised themselves in all the other things that hadn't been thought of quite yet, like bedsteads and bagpipes and bonfires, not to mention violins, cricket bats, toothpicks, clothes pegs, chopsticks and misericords. Men and women would sit in the shade of trees, reading books, and the trees, dreaming of all that was to come, saw that they were the books as well as the chairs the men and women sat in, and the combs in the women's hair, and the shiny handles of the muskets, and the hoops the children chased across the lawns. The trees took pride in the idea of being a book: they thought a book was a noble thing to become, if you had to become anything – a terrible bore to be a rafter, after all, and a wheel would mean such a battering, though of course the travel was a bonus, and what tree in its right mind would wish to be rack, coffin, crucifix, gallows...

One tree was more excited than all the rest, and that was the ash. The ash has such an inviting, feathery shade: when men and women first had books to take into the shade of trees, they often chose the shade of an ash. The ash would look down at these people reading and see that they were discovering new regions inside themselves, and notice how when they stood up and left the jurisdiction of its branches they had changed as if buds inside them were coming into leaf, and the ash saw that this change was a property of the marks on the paper, and that paper was the only leaf with worlds in it. Soon ash trees were discussing this phenomenon all over the place, whispering about books in Manchuria and Poland and the Pennines, passing information from grove to grove, until ash trees across North America and the Eastern and Western Palearctic were sighing and swaying with thoughts of words and pens and poems and printing presses and Odysseus and Scheherazade and the *Song of Songs...*

So ash trees dreamed of becoming books themselves one day, even though they would be much in demand as firewood, and prized as material for oars, hockey sticks and the chassis frames of Morgan motor cars. Sometimes, dreaming ahead, they saw men and women sitting beneath them, writing – writing in notebooks and diaries, writing letters of love and consolation, writing stories. And the ash tree wanted to be that, too – not just the book, but the writing in it, the words that carried the worlds. They saw the men and women holding their pens, and the ink that came out of them onto the paper, and although they didn't have hands, they tried to curl their branches into fingers that might hold pens, and they dreamed it so vividly that the tips of their fingers turned black with ink as they waved against the blank white page of the sky, trying to write on it.

Look closely: the ash tree has black buds, and the branches bend upwards at their tips, towards the whiteness.

The Quaking of the Aspen
James Robertson

The aspen is known in Scottish Gaelic as *an critheann* (the trembling tree) and in Scots as the *quakin esp* or *quakin ash*. Mythology associates it, like the rowan, with the netherworld of the fairies: it was believed that the aspen had magical properties that could encourage eloquence or even restore the faculty of speech...

The Laird of Logie took himself a wife, and she was the Laird of Kittlespindie's daughter. Now Kittlespindie was a wealthy man, and Logie was not, so there was policy in Logie's wooing of her but little else. Perhaps the girl suspected this and, understandably, resented it. At any rate, something was amiss with her, for from the day she crossed Logie's door not a word issued from her lips. Nobody could tell if she was truly struck dumb or just plain thrawn; nor, if she was playing tricks, could anyone catch her out at it.

Several months of this caused Logie to become utterly dejected, and he took to walking the moors just to be out of the house, which itself seemed half-suffocated by his wife's silence. One day as he walked, a tiny, beautiful lady came riding across the moor. She was wearing a green silk dress, her hair was bedecked with ribbons, and bells were braided into the mane of her horse. She stopped and asked why he looked so downcast. Was he not the Laird of Logie that had lately taken Kittlespindie's bonnie daughter for his bride?

Logie felt an urgent need to confess his anguish and his sense of guilt, even though he had never seen the lady before. 'You are right,' he said, 'but I married her for greed, not love, and now she does not speak, and I believe my deceit is the cause of her sickness.'

'It is a sickness easily cured,' the lady said. 'You must go to the glen where the aspen stands, and take a single leaf from it. When your bride is asleep tonight, lay the leaf under her tongue. In the morning her speech will be restored.'

The lady rode on her way, and Logie set off for the glen, but as he went he thought to himself that the stranger had probably not understood how total his wife's silence was. And so, to be sure that the cure was effective, he brought back three aspen leaves. That evening he was impatient for bedtime. When at last his wife fell asleep he carefully placed the leaves under her tongue.

In the morning he woke first, removed the leaves and then waited anxiously to see what would happen. Kittlespindie's daughter woke with a yawn and immediately began to complain. 'What a terrible, restless night I've had! I've hardly slept at all.' 'Oh, no,' he said, who had lain awake most of the night, 'you never stirred once. And look, you can speak!' He tried to hug her in his happiness, but she pushed him away. 'Speak?' she cried. 'What are you on about? Of course I can speak.' And indeed she could. In fact she hardly drew breath, first scolding him for his foolishness, then rushing on without pause on every subject, both trivial and profound, as if all the words she had not uttered for months were bursting from her at once. Logie expected the torrent to diminish after an hour or so, but on the contrary it seemed to increase, and her words became ever more confused and deafening.

Desperate to get away from his now too-voluble spouse, he hurried out to the moor with the aspen leaves crushed in his fist. To his surprise, the same green-gowned lady came riding by. 'You did not follow my instructions,' she said, when Logie told her what had happened. 'Now you must take those leaves back to the tree and bury them beneath its roots. And this time do exactly as I say.'

Logie obeyed, digging a hole at the foot of the quaking tree and burying the leaves in it. When he returned home, he found his wife restored to health, speaking neither too much nor too little, and he embraced and kissed her and resolved to love and respect her for the rest of their days. And so he did, and they grew happy and old together.

Each year, he would visit the quaking tree when its new foliage appeared, and sit below it for a while. There was a strange comfort to him in the ceaseless whispering on the branches above his head. He would think of the green lady, whose wisdom had been so useful to him but whom he had never seen again. And then he would go back home to his wife.

To this day the aspen's leaves are sometimes known as 'old wives' tongues,' a name that springs, perhaps, from some such tale as this.

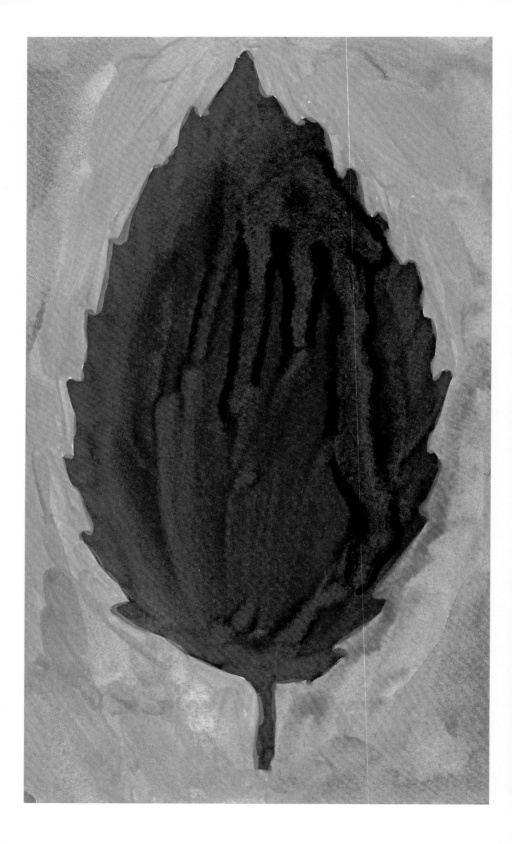

Why Nothing Grows Under the Beech (or Does It?)
Richard Mabey

To say that the surface of the world was bleak long ago would be an understatement – though 'under' was not an idea people understood very well then. The land was hot and flat and stony. Nothing grew more than the height of a hand above the surface. There were no bushes, no trees, no shade under the sun. The people who lived on the surface – let's call them Surfs – were roasted and bored in equal measure. They sucked juice from excruciatingly prickly cactus. They nibbled mushrooms as dry as crisps. They banged stones together to relieve the monotony. They had no words for any of these things, and the noises they made were the ooohs and clacks of gloom and frustration.

The two Surfs who were about to change the face of the world – let's call them Rip and Wave, since they didn't have names for themselves either – mooned about, picking little threads of parched lichen to give each other. It was the one pretty custom of their miserable lives: they rose up on tiptoe and passed the threads from mouth to mouth. Often they would burrow down into the ground to shelter from the sun, and hold hands below the sand.

What they didn't know was that, just a few feet below them, other creatures were also holding hands – or maybe we should say tendrils – under the ground. Let's call them Subs. They were round and truffle-like, and were all joined together as a kind of underground tribe by their tendrils. They nibbled at buried leaves and dead insects, but mainly lived off whatever mites of nourishment the rain washed out of the earth. They were pale and shadowy and ached for the light of the sun.

One day, to pass the time, Rip and Wave began a game of bashing the ground with stones, and mimicking the sounds they made. 'Blairch,' mouthed Rip, as he swiped the rocks, and imitated the clatter of the fragments as they scattered like shrapnel. 'Burp,' replied Wave, crashing her rock straight down into the sand so that it billowed up as a great puff of air. 'Belch,' countered Rip. 'Bach,' Wave tried, surprising herself with a delicate rendition of sand crystals tinkling. 'Bark!' Rip barked back. Then they dashed their stones down together, deep into the sand. 'Beeeeeech!' they yelled.

Rip and Wave's stones broke down into the world of the Subs, letting light into their dark and gloomy world. Those touched by the light sniffed the air, felt the warmth and shot up towards it as if they'd been yanked by a magnet. As the tendrils rose up, they began to swell, and their skin became grey and smooth. In a short while they were as tall as a Surf, and began to sprout twiggy growths, as if they had turned into a living fountain. Soon the twigs, delirious in the brightness, grew green leafy tips that caught the sunlight, turned it into food and passed it down to the listless Subs left behind.

Rip and Wave's mouths gaped in amazement at what they had conjured up. 'Beech' was the noise that came out. Don't believe what they say about the word becoming flesh. The word became wood.

Rip and Wave revelled in the shade of the beech. It was cool and airy, and the sun flickering between the leaves made the crown of the tree look like a dark sky full of stars.

Rip and Wave held hands again (above ground this time) and invented many new noises, and scratched their shapes on the soft bark of the beech. Occasionally what they wrote made new things happen, just as when they conjured the beech up from the ground. Once they used their stones to draw pictures of themselves, and as the great tree grew, their pictures fused together. Many ages later, when writing on beeches was common, a wise man made a proverb: 'As these letters grow, so will our love.'

The remaining Subs were happy too. They received gifts of food from the leaves of the beech tree, and gave back to it the special, stony nourishments they took from the soil. To this day not much grows on the soil beneath a beech tree, and people think of it as a dead, dark space. But, as the wise Surfs understood, this is the view of those who see things only as surfaces, and are blind to the bright thread of life that joins the beings below ground with the beech above, and which stretches right up to the sun itself.

Why Birches Have Silver Bark
Tracy Chevalier

Birch trees did not always have silver bark. There was a time when their trunks were the grey-brown of most other trees. It was sex that changed things. It always does.

Long ago a girl grew up in a village surrounded by thick forests full of all sorts of trees: elm, ash, beech, birch, oak, rowan, hawthorn, hornbeam. She loved trees and knew the forest well.

Unfortunately the girl's parents were very strict and would not allow her to have a boyfriend. The men in the village were not good enough for her, they felt.

The girl was less picky and more hormonal. One day she arranged to meet a man. 'Come to the ash grove north of the village at midnight,' she whispered to him as they drew water from the village well. He nodded, too ashamed to admit he had no idea what an ash tree looked like. Instead he crashed about in the woods for an hour before giving up and going home.

'He's too interested in football to care about me,' the girl thought, and set her sights on another. 'Meet me at the stand of beech trees east of the village,' she instructed as they were buying bread at the baker's. This man also knew more about sports than trees, and didn't even get beyond the willows at the edge of the village before he turned back.

The girl decided to make it as easy as possible for her next potential lover. 'Do you know the old oak that stands on its own in the middle of the woods to the south of the village?' she said as they waited for their flour to be ground at the village mill. 'Meet me there.' Surely everyone knows what an oak looks like. But no: the man stood under a lone elm, wondering if its wood would make a good cricket bat.

The girl waited under the oak tree and wept at the thought of dying a virgin. 'My parents are right,' she sobbed. 'The village men are too stupid for me!'

She gave up on men then, until one day a stranger arrived. Not only was he handsome, but he also didn't care much for sports, turning down the chance to play five-a-side football or cricket on the village green. Instead he wove the girl a daisy chain. She took this as a good sign, and invited him to meet her, though she decided to test him on his tree knowledge. Only a tree-loving man would do. 'Meet me in the birch wood to the west of the village,' she commanded.

The man agreed. Unfortunately, however, he was from the city, where even fewer people knew about trees. And being a man, he wouldn't admit he couldn't tell a birch from a beech. He simply trusted fate: if they were meant to be together, he would find her.

Now, the birch trees had already had some of the other suitors stumble through them on their abortive rendezvous, so when the girl came to wait among them, they knew what might happen. Indeed, as it grew late and the man did not arrive, the girl began to weep.

Then the moon appeared from behind a cloud, lighting up the forest. Among the birches there was one tree with mutant genes that had made its bark a silvery white. The other birches had often teased it for being different, but on this night its difference became its strength, for when the moonlight struck it, it lit up like a beacon in the dark forest. Seeing its glow, the man made straight for it and there found the girl.

She was so relieved to have a lover at last that, in her post-coital bliss, she vowed to protect the silver birch from ever being chopped down. This protected status ensured not only its long life, but its propagation as well. After a time, silver birches became the norm.

They are still the best trees for a tryst.

This One (or How the Blackthorn Got Its Flowers)
Susan Elderkin

On the day that the gifts were handed out the blackthorn was late. By the time it got there, the gate was shut and a sign had been put up saying 'Creation complete.' The blackthorn considered leaving a note on the gatepost, but decided there wasn't much point. Back then, all the trees were stemmy and green and unformed, and the blackthorn was happy as it was. So it went back to the woods and thought no more about it.

As time passed, and winter became spring and

spring turned into summer, it became clear to the blackthorn that all the other trees had something about them that people loved. The beeches and oaks were the best trees for climbing, and some small child always seemed to be hauling itself up into their branches. Other children ran to hide within the encircling fronds of the weeping willow. The slender silver birch was undeniably sexy. The aspen had a fragile, trembling thing going on. People were forever setting up their easels in front of a flowering wild cherry. The horse chestnut had its conkers, the oak its cute acorn cup-and-saucer routine, the sycamore its clever-clogs helicopters. But what did the blackthorn have? Bare stems, and short ones at that.

The tree grew more and more depressed. Its stems began to blacken and turn inwards. On windy days, the other trees heard its dry, grieving rattle.

'No children,' said the rattle. 'Not tall like other trees.'

A breeze rippled the handsome leaves of the maple. 'Ahem – tree, did you say? *Tree?* Thicket, surely.'

One blackthorn branch creaked against another.

Overhead, a eucalyptus fluttered its grey leaves to show their pretty white undersides. 'Get over it,' it tutted. 'I didn't get where I am today by whinging. I got here–'

'In a trouser turn-up!' bellowed a chorus of trees as the wind surged through their canopies. 'Yeah, we know.'

The blackthorn listened to the waves of laughter, and a full understanding of genetic gifts grew inside it, of short straws and long straws, and the price you pay for being late. Bitterness mingled with its sadness, and the following year from out of this bitterness the blackthorn developed spines on its branches, strong enough to rip the shirt or skin of anyone who dared brush up against it. Another year it produced fat, purple berries so sour and astringent that anyone who tasted one immediately spat it out and turned away in disgust. Its branches became denser and denser, even tangled. The blackthorn was making things worse, but didn't know how to stop.

'Keep away from that tree,' the blackthorn heard a mother say to her little girl, one cold-snap day towards the end of winter. A stubby, hard-bellied dog was sniffing around the blackthorn's roots. 'You too, Poppy, come away,' she called to the dog.

The dog glanced up at the blackthorn, recognised

another loser in the gene-allocation game, then cocked its leg and let loose a warm stream against the tree's trunk. But the blackthorn didn't care. It had eyes only for the little girl. With her red hair streaming from under her Dublin-green hat – colours that the blackthorn had long admired in the holly – she was the most delightful creature it had ever seen.

'This one?' she asked her mother. She came and stood before the blackthorn, looking up at it with her open, enquiring face.

'Yes, this one, this one,' the blackthorn intoned in the language of trees, every woody fibre of its being bristling. As it drank in the sight of the little girl, all the longing and loneliness it had ever known welled and surged in its sap, from the ends of its roots up into the tough, unpliable rods that squeezed and stoppered its ardent soul. It wanted only one thing: to find something from deep within itself to hold this girl's gaze, to spark her interest, her love, her joy – to make her come back, again and again. Something that wouldn't tear at her tender skin, or dry out her tongue. Something from before the time when the gate had been closed, from when the blackthorn was young and new and existed simply of greenness and a hunger for water and light. From when it knew nothing of gifts that were bestowed and not bestowed. As the sap rose and swelled within its stiffened branches, the tips of the blackthorn's twigs burst into a sudden shower of tiny white flowers, delicate as stars. The effect was of a billowing cloud that, on this particular day – with winter on the back foot, but before spring had fully stepped in to take its place – was quite the loveliest thing in the woods.

The girl smiled at the blackthorn's blossom, her little face aglow with surprise, and for the next few weeks, whenever she came to walk in the woods, she drew her mother's attention to the pretty tree with the flowers. In time the mother's feelings towards the prickly blackthorn softened, and one day she even brought gloves and a pair of secateurs, cut a tall flowering stem with several offshoots, and carried it home to put in a vase. The blackthorn got to experience the downside of being loved, of one limb being brutally severed from another, the slow agony of dehydration; but it was worth it. And although today the blackthorn is still inclined to become somewhat gloomy over the winter months, it never fails to lift its own and others' spirits when it comes into bloom very early in the spring. And on windy days, those who know the language of trees can make out its creaking, raspy saw from within the noisome orchestra of the woods.

Listen. Do you hear it?

That one.

The Cuckoo and the Cherry Tree
Rachel Billington

The wild cherry tree is a hermaphrodite, both male and female, and more than a little poisonous. This didn't stop the cuckoo falling in love with him (and her). It happened a very long time ago when the cuckoo was almost unknown, a plain, meek bird who produced only the smallest cheep when spoken to.

The cuckoo loved with true passion the cherry tree's silky purplish-pink trunk, its cascade of wedding-white flowers, its red and luscious fruit.

'You are the tree of my dreams,' she cheeped, aroused for the first time to flights of fancy.

Sadly, the cherry tree did not reciprocate such feelings. 'Get off, can't you,' it replied rudely. 'You're always hanging round here and it's getting on my nerves.'

'I'm only admiring you,' peeped the cuckoo, deeply hurt.

'Then don't sit on me,' answered the cherry, shaking its branches about in an attempt to dislodge her. 'Your ugly mug is putting off other prettier birds.'

'Like who?' twittered the cuckoo, clinging on tight.

'Like the blackbird, the goldfinch, the great tit, the woodchat, the chaffinch, the yellowhammer. They all have gumption, too. Even the sparrow has more gumption than you. Being so beautiful myself, I like a bird with a bit of go.'

If the cuckoo had not been so in love and so without gumption, she might have pecked off the tree's delicate flowers with her sharp, curved beak. Instead she flew away and hid in the middle of a hawthorn tree while she considered her beloved's cruel words.

Her mood was not improved when she heard

how all the other birds were laughing at her discomfiture, showing off with their most elaborate trills and arpeggios. Even a far-off chicken cackled, and a passing owl hooted derisively. Worst of all was the lark, who laughed in an endlessly ascending scale of notes.

The humiliation, however, gave her an idea. She was, as it happened, ready to lay an egg. This was usually a trying time because, being not at all talented at do-it-yourself, she had never mastered the art of nest-making. Half the time, her eggs fell through the nest and smashed on the ground.

Now, in one fell swoop, she would take her revenge on those mocking little birds and turn herself into just the sort of girl the wild cherry – not called 'wild' for nothing – would admire. That evening, she flew and hopped her way to a neat little nest, presently occupied by four little blue eggs but having just room for one more rather larger.

'Now *I've* got gumption!' the cuckoo exulted, flapping her wings.

Soon the cuckoo was the talk of the coppice. Now that the flowers of the wild cherry had given way to the fruit, a multitude of pretty little birds were gathered on its branches to peck at the cherries and complain loudly.

'I'd only been gone a moment and there it was, a great big ugly egg,' tweeted an outraged tit.

'You must push it out!' shrilled a large blackbird.

'I could never do that,' fluted the sweet voice of the willow warbler. 'Give it to me. I shall foster it and bring it up as my own.'

'It'll eat you out of nest and home,' warned the tit.

The wild cherry listened to them with its branches waving. It had never heard of any bird pulling such a fast one before. The cuckoo's wickedness and guile excited the tree more and more. The bird would never be better than ugly, but handsome is as handsome does.

The next time the cuckoo flew nearby, the cherry tree dangled a bunch of fruit in front of her and whispered, 'You're quite a girl, I must say.' It gently undulated its branches. 'You'll find the sweetest cherries near the back. A little more to the left. That's it.'

As the cuckoo pecked, she felt her chest swell with pride. Suddenly a huge new song burst from her beak. 'Cuckoo! Cuckoo! Cuckoo!'

'*Ravissante*, my crazy darling.' The wild cherry swung her fruit in rhythm. 'So individual. So arresting. You might almost say masculine. I wouldn't be surprised if it made you famous.'

'Ah, my love,' responded the cuckoo, trying to sound modest, 'without you, I would still be that dull, unknown bird, instead of a devil-may-care *chanteuse* with a big voice. I shall pay you the compliment of opening my beak for my first glorious "Cuckoo!" of the year at the very same moment you pop open your first exquisite flower.'

'Charming!' exclaimed the cherry tree. Bird and tree were lost in mutual admiration.

So it is that each year the cuckoo sings for the first time just as the first blossoms burst open on the wild cherry, and we all rejoice and cry out, 'Spring is here!'

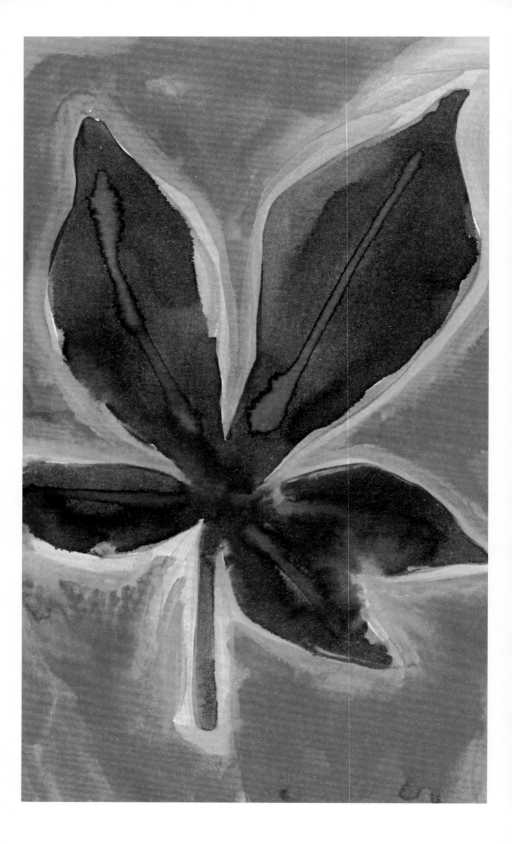

Why the Chestnut Tree Has White Candles
Blake Morrison

For a few weeks every spring, the chestnut blazes with white candles. Their flames are so bright you have to shade your eyes when you look at them. Then they gutter and die, and their blooms drip to the earth like wax – until they catch light again next spring. A miracle of nature, people say. But the chestnut tree's candles didn't come naturally.

It happened like this.

Once upon a time all was darkness. Then Zeus threw his hat in the ring, and there was light for half the day. All the creatures of the earth were delighted. But soon they wanted more. Why should the sun disappear each dusk? Light our nights for us as well, they begged Zeus.

Zeus was having none of it. A god can only take so much. If they wanted their nights lit up, they must sort it out themselves.

Hamm and Hermione volunteered to help. Both had been born with a special gift – winged arms and feet. It was said their mothers had mated with swans. Whatever the truth, the two children became friends and, as they grew up, would often soar above the earth together for a laugh. Now it was time to spread their wings in earnest.

It was Hermione who dreamt up the plan. Out in the sky were millions of stars. All it needed was to bring one down to earth, or as near to earth as people could stand, so that it hovered there, like a paper lantern, lighting up the night.

'But how will we do it?' Hamm said.

'You'll take one side and I'll take the other and we'll pull.'

'Will we be strong enough?'

'Of course. There's only air in our way. It'll be a doddle.'

'But even if we succeed, what's to stop the star drifting off again?'

'We'll tie it to a giant tree trunk.'

They set off next day for the nearest star, but when they got there it proved too hot to handle – so hot their wings were scorched and they had to wait till the feathers grew back. Things looked hopeless. Was every star as fiery as the sun? Then they came upon a star they hadn't noticed before. It was perfect: small, cool, phosphorescent, and light as an eggshell. When they pulled, it came with them, easy as pie.

'Take care,' Hermione said. 'It's terribly fragile.' She was right. No other star in the cosmos was as delicate. As they carried it, little fragments broke off and slipped away into the night, shining back at them like glow-worms.

For an age, Hamm and Hermione headed downwards, back to earth. Strong though they were, and light though the star was, the journey was exhausting. Sometimes they pushed from behind; sometimes they rowed, using their free arms like oars; sometimes they swam on their backs, kicking their legs, with the star like a giant beach ball above them.

As they descended, they looked like a pair of divers with a huge white jellyfish, bright bubbles trailing behind.

Slowly the earth rose into sight below.

Though friends, Hamm and Hermione didn't always see eye to eye. As they neared the end of their journey, they began to argue.

'Let's get this over with,' Hamm said, yanking so hard that a large slice of star sheared off. 'We're going too slow.'

'If we go any faster, it will shatter,' Hermione said.

'I want to get home. I'm tired and hungry.'

'Just be patient.'

Hamm tried to be patient, but as the earth swam closer – so close that he could make out rivers, forests and plains, clear as a football pitch under floodlights – he couldn't help rushing. The star twisted and bulged as he humped it like a coal sack over his shoulders.

'Slow down, we're close enough,' Hermione said. It was where they'd planned to stop: there were mountains not far below. All it needed was for one of them to fly down and fetch a rope while the other held the star steady. Then they'd tether it to a giant tree trunk and their mission would be done.

'Stop!' Hermione cried. But Hamm pressed on, not looking where he was going. The star creaked and groaned like a ship on a raging sea.

'Stop, stop!' she shouted, seeing a peak right below them. But it was too late. As they brushed the snow-capped summit, there was a rumble from within the star, then cracks spreading across its crust, and a terrific explosion, like the shattering of an icicle or a conker. The lightshow that followed was spectacular, as zillions of star-chunks drifted out into the night like fire balloons. As they faded, darkness returned to earth.

Every star fragment was lost, except one, which caught in Hermione's hair. It might have stayed there forever, like a halo, but in her confusion she flew into the branches of a chestnut tree. And though she came to no harm, the star halo fell off and broke into tiny pieces.

Each piece became a candle and lodged in the branches of the chestnut tree, where the flames burn brightly to this day. The candles begin as sticky buds in spring, and in autumn they become conkers. But for a few glorious weeks in May they blaze like the star Hamm and Hermione so nearly brought back to earth.

Why Crab Apples Are Sour
Maria McCann

Long after the expulsion of humans, a flock of birds went winging through Eden, touching down here and there, picking and pecking wherever they chose. They settled on the Tree of Knowledge, where the boldest bird filled its beak with apple flesh and seeds. The flock flew off again, carefree and careless, darting close to the very edge of Eden, until at last the boldest strayed, for an instant, over the garden wall. The bird was at once buffeted by wind and pelted with hail. Cawing with fear, it dropped the apple flesh into the chaos of the outside world, where it sank deep into mud. The bird fled back to the perfumed trees and crystal springs of the garden where the inhabitants were innocent, the weather was predictable and nothing ever changed.

Down in the ooze the pips took root. It was bitterly cold, just the other side of the wall of Eden. The saplings that struggled up were twisted and half-starved, and their fruit soured by sadness: they were, after all, offspring of the Tree of Knowledge and they had suffered their own Fall. But Knowledge is also the Knowledge of What Might Be, and each seed carried within it a germ of hope: that from experience might come wisdom. The more stunted and wretched the little trees, the more mouth-puckering their fruit, the more they clung to life. Through thousands of years they seeded and multiplied, their twigs infested with mistletoe, their trunks bent, their bark sun-blistered. They were waiting for some sign that though Eden was lost, Knowledge had at least been gained; that people were sadder but wiser too, and so, in time, things might come round.

After many centuries a holy man and his servant passed a hedge full of crab apple trees. 'The fruit of this tree is accursed,' said the holy man, 'having caused the downfall of our first parents. Hence its Latin name, *Malus*. Bad.'

The trees heard this and saw the look of blame cast upon them by both master and servant. Their apples grew a little sourer.

More time passed. A woman and her son came to the hedge one September when the crab trees were heavy with fruit.

'Climb up there,' said the woman. 'Throw them down to me.'

'They're sour,' said the boy.

His mother smiled. 'Good things can be made from sour apples.'

The boy shinned up the tree and the apples began to sweeten a little.

The centuries flew by (though to the human beings, battling on, they seemed to crawl) and suddenly everything was evolution, evolution, evolution. No such thing, now, as a bad species: *malus* meant simply *apple*, and survival was the ultimate good.

'Who has survived longer than we have?' mused the crab apples, preparing for recognition. But humans, who craved sweetness without limit, were now busy breeding new varieties, johnny-come-lately fruit, and barely noticed their old companions. The crab apples faded into the uncultivated places, of interest only to unimportant people. There they continued their ancient cycle of blossom, fruit and death.

A couple sat under a flowering crab apple tree.

'I was wrong,' said the man. The tree put forth a few more petals.

The woman said, 'You were…but so was I,' and the petals glittered in the spring sun.

The next time the woman came there she was alone. She sat beneath the tree and gazed over the fields. The crop had been poor and she had a child coming. After a while she noticed some crab apples lying in the grass nearby. She sighed: they were so small and sour.

The tree silently held out its branches.

'Anything's better than nothing,' the woman thought. She filled her pockets with fruit and went home to make crab apple jelly. As she stood over the pan, she felt something move in her for the first time. She put her hand on her belly, vowing she would never beat the child as she had been beaten. Her stove was smoky, her pan dented and her spoon bent, yet as she stirred and skimmed she was working a universal magic: the ancient art of bringing forth sweet out of sour, of reclaiming and redeeming, making good out of *malus*.

Once, before the Fall, apples were luscious as peaches. Some people think that in time we will all become wise, perfect solutions will be found to our problems and Eden will come again. On that day the crab apples will return to their original sweetness. Until then, as the patching up and struggling on continue, crab apples remain what they have been for so long: fruits of which something hopeful can be made, Trees of Knowledge.

Why Elms Die Young
Terence Blacker

As any carpenter knows, elm is a tricky wood to work – robust and beautiful, but also recalcitrant and unpredictable. Even when it has been dried, it will continue to move, rebelling against the role the craftsman has given it.

There is a reason for this excess of individuality. All trees in the forest are proud but, with the elm, pride tips – some would say unacceptably – into arrogance.

It took several millennia for other trees to acknowledge that the attitude of the elm was becoming a problem. The forest is a tolerant, live-and-let-live sort of place, where there is a general sense that trees should not judge one another but concentrate on their own growing.

The arrogance of the elm, though, eventually became impossible to ignore. There were murmurings among the trees. Finally it was agreed that the ash, which has an easygoing sort of authority about it, would address the issue.

'The thing is this,' the ash said to the elm. 'All of the trees in the forest have individual strengths, and we all get along pretty well. The alder provides wood that hardens with water. The blackthorn protects animals with its spiky branches. The oak provides the mighty timber for ships and houses. In my own modest way, I produce wood which I believe is rather useful for firewood.'

'Your point being?' asked the elm.

'It's simply that all trees have their functions. To be candid, we've been wondering what gives you the right to behave as if you are superior to the rest of us.'

'I am elm,' said the elm.

This reply did not go down well in the forest.

'What kind of answer is that?' muttered the hazel.

'I am hornbeam,' said the hornbeam. 'So what?

Statement of identity hardly constitutes a reason.'

The elm seemed to have lost interest in the conversation. When it did speak again, it was in a tone of weary contempt.

'I am elm.'

The matter was dropped for a few centuries, but discontent grew among the other trees. It was the willow who one day suggested that something had to be done.

'But what?' sighed the ash. 'It is elm. End of story.'

'I have friends – don't press me for details,' said the willow. 'I could have a word.'

The trees agreed that little harm could come from the willow talking to its friends, and thought no more about it.

The willow knew a beetle that had recently travelled from Asia. When the willow explained its problems, the beetle seemed interested.

'When does the elm start misbehaving?' it asked.

'When it becomes an adult tree,' said the willow. 'It's quite reasonable when it is young, but as soon as it starts appearing above the hawthorn, the rowan, the hazel and the other small trees, its behaviour becomes impossible.'

'I think I may be able to help,' said the beetle.

A few years later, the trees began to notice that something unexpected was happening. As soon as young elms reached a certain height, above the hawthorn, the rowan, the hazel and other small trees, their bark became clogged with fungus and, quite soon afterwards, they died.

It was upsetting.

'I think the elm has learned its lesson,' the ash said one day to the willow. 'Maybe you could have another word with your friends.'

The beetle was surprisingly unhelpful.

'These things are cyclical,' it said. 'One day, the elm will develop resistance to the fungus. Give it a few centuries and it will be back up there with the big boys. Thank you very much for the gig, by the way.'

To its credit, the elm has never complained about its fate. Every year, its roots spread, and its suckers burst through the earth. It grows and grows, knowing full well that, at the very moment when other trees reach their most useful years, it will inevitably wither and die.

In woodland, even now, you can hear its refrain – hopeful, defiant, despairing, quieter than it once was.

I am elm.

I am elm.

I am elm.

Never Cut a Hawthorn
Joanne Harris

On the sunny side of Red Horse Hill, in the corner of a field, there stands an ancient hawthorn tree. No one knows how old it is; no one – not even the other trees – remembers a time when it was young. Most of it is already dead; but a single living branch survives, blossoming in springtime, producing a handful of haws in autumn, when the leaves turn.

The fallow field in which it stands belongs to a woman who lives alone. She is old; has always been old. Her hands are clumps of twisted branch. Her hair is white as blossom. Her skin is brown and cracked, and her eyes are bright as haws in the sun. Every day, rain or shine, she sits in her rocking chair on her porch, and sometimes she sings, and sometimes she sews, and sometimes seems to fall asleep, though anyone watching closely would see that her eyes are never *quite* shut, and are always fixed on the hawthorn tree that stands in the corner of the field.

She remembers a time when she was young, many, many years ago. She does not count the years any more, but marks the seasons as they pass, in blossom and leaf, in fruit and fall. *Mae* was her name in those distant days, and everybody loved her.

Everybody? No, not quite. One young man never noticed her. He lived alone in a tiny cottage on the far side of the fallow field, and seldom spoke to anyone. Folk called him *Thorn*, for his surliness, and avoided him whenever they could. And the girl, being stubborn, being female, had set her heart on that young man. But the more she pursued him, the less he cared, and the less he seemed to notice her.

Now the hawthorn tree that stood in Thorn's field had a reputation. Folk claimed it brought both good and ill luck. It was said that the fairies haunted it, that its flowers should never enter the house; that to fall asleep in its shadow could send a person staring mad.

But most of all, the fairy tree was said to be the heart's tree, a tree for lovers and for love. This was what brought Mae to the field, on May Eve at midnight, to pick a handful of hawthorn blooms and make them into a May Day crown, so that Thorn would know her love at last and smile at her in the morning.

But in the morning, the young man was as distant and surly as ever. Summer came, and the hawthorn tree lost its bloom and burst into leaf, and still Mae longed for him to look at her – just once – and smile. And so she crept back to the fairy tree on Midsummer's Eve at midnight, and cut a swatch of thorny stems and made herself a green May ball to hang outside her window in the hope that her love would see it, and know.

But on Midsummer's Day the young man remained as silent and thorny as ever. And so Mae went to Crazy Nan, who lived at the edge of the forest, and who was mad, and spoke with the fairies, and slept under hedges, and would know what to do.

Crazy Nan listened to her, and smiled a little smile to herself.

Then she said: 'You want his heart? Then go to the fairy tree at Samhain, on the night when all the dead are awake, and cut yourself a nice big piece out of the living heart of the tree. Make it into a charm, my girl, to wear around your pretty neck. After that, he'll belong to you.'

Mae did as old Nan said, and crept back home on All Hallows' Eve with a piece of the green heart of the tree in her apron pocket. And in the morning she went running to the cottage across the field, certain that this time, she would find love waiting.

But when Mae arrived at the cottage door, no one answered. She went in and found Thorn lying on the ground, his shirt soaked through with his heart's blood. Horrified, Mae understood that the young man and the tree were one, and that her love was dying. She ran to the fairy tree and gave back the piece that she had cut, and bound it with strips torn from her skirts, strips of red flannel that fluttered and flew.

When she returned to the cottage, Thorn was gone. Some say the fairies took him away; no one knows for certain.

In any case, the tree survived. It stands there to this day, and folk still deck it with ribbons and bows, and the old woman tells this story. Of course, there's no telling whether it's true. But just in case it is, beware – never cut a hawthorn tree, or bring the flowers into the house; for love can send a person mad just as soon as sorcery, and it's wiser by far, the old folk say, to have nothing to do with either.

Why Holly Berries Are as Red as Roses
Philippa Gregory

No one plants a holly tree, so darkly green and prickly. So where do they come from? They grow everywhere, every park and hedge has a holly, as if the day-to-day park and hedge and neglected garden need such a night-time mystery, embedded in the ordinary. I look around my little winter-blasted garden and feel powerless at the sight of the holly tree that leans against my house, reaching nearly to the roof, grey bark as smooth as a slowworm, leaves impenetrable as a hedgehog, green, green as death.

I shall have to get a tree surgeon to prune it; better still, grub it up. Its great head is pressed against my bedroom window, its stringy roots wind like snakes around the foundations of my little town house. I live here alone now, nobody cares for me, I cannot be enwrapped in living wood.

The sorrow started without reason at the end of summer and it makes me slow and stupid now, like a chilled bee lost without flowers. I cannot sleep at night for the constant seep of grief, I have taken to crying in my sleep, and I cannot wake in the day, nor taste food nor bear the light. My friends say that I must make an effort; as if happiness comes when called. I went to the doctor, and he said he would give me a drug that would ease the pain, but it turned out that it eased everything, hope as well as sorrow, and left me dull as well as sad. Now I am like an old woman, fearful of the approaching darkness, mumbling with fear.

Tomorrow I shall telephone for a man to come and cut down the holly tree, tomorrow I will force myself to go somewhere bright and noisy, drag myself into light. I must fell my sorrow and tear out its roots, I must cut it out of me.

That night I dream of the holly tree. In my dream he is both tree and man, he is King Holly and he slides up the sash window of my bedroom and steps over the sill, sure of his welcome. He lies with me and I cannot resist him, his mouth scratches my lips; and my naked body, white as the moon, is burnished red as a holly berry under the prickle of his touch till I cry out in joy and take the green-scented darkness of him deep into me and his roots wrap around my bare feet and I sigh with a pleasure that is the other side of pain.

In the morning I wake early, as the winter light shines in my window and I know myself to be different, I feel whole. I go downstairs to the kitchen and set the kettle to boil and look out at the garden. A robin is singing in the boughs of the holly tree, singing as if for joy inside the darkness of the leaves, eyeing the scarlet of the berries with his bright eager gaze. It is so early that the moon still sits on the rooftops like a circular mirror of the rising white sun. The round moon and the round sun face each other in the pale arc of the sky, as if night and day are the same thing – either side of the same sky like the same coin, as if sorrow and joy are one. And I understand this, at last.

The Stickiness of Lime Trees
Catherine O'Flynn

There were eighty lime trees in Linden Road. Despite their number and elaborate seasonal costume changes, no one in the road paid attention to the trees. The young man from number 54 had once, for no clear reason, stuck a kitchen knife in the tree outside his front door, but apart from him, nobody seemed to notice them.

The trees, though, noticed the people. They watched them with great interest, exchanging theories about their comings and goings, sometimes guessing at their motivations and desires, always looking for an opportunity to help with the many challenges the people faced.

The trees were proud of the successes they had enjoyed in their efforts to help. People were careless and clumsy, always letting things slip through their soft fingers, and the trees made it their business to make sure these things were not lost. They carefully stored empty crisp packets, old chicken bones and soggy gloves in the shoots around the base of their trunks for when their owners would need them again. They caught flimsy polythene bags and cardigans in their branches when they floated from cars or were hurled from windows. One tree had held a sock high in her branches for over fifteen years and had no intention of letting go of it any time soon.

Long ago the trees had noticed how few of the people went outside when the weather turned chilly, and so they combined their efforts to fill the colourless autumn gardens with their beautiful golden heart-shaped leaves. The trees delighted in seeing the people stumble out into the light and gather the leaves into large black sacks day after day. The people needed so much help.

Occasionally the trees would turn their attention to someone in particular who seemed to need extra help. Tili, the tree outside number 42, was concerned about its occupant. She liked to call him Ray, though she didn't know his name. Ray left in his car every day when the birds were singing in Tili's branches, and he returned with the birds each evening, though he was never heard to sing. Tili saw Ray through the uncurtained window watching television programmes about the big war that had happened back in olden times. She told the other trees that Ray had eight complete part-work magazine serials with accompanying DVDs all about the war, and the trees all agreed that was a lot. Tili said that another person with flowing hair and blue shoes used to live at number 42 but left one day, shouting and crying and pulling a suitcase with a broken wheel.

Now Ray was on his own. He still went out each day and returned home each evening to learn about aerial dogfights or escape attempts from notorious prison camps, but through the window Tili saw the times when Ray would pause the DVD, put his head on his arms, and be very still. She wanted very much to reassure Ray of her constant leafy presence, to gently kiss his soft fingers and say, 'I have not abandoned you.' She spoke to the aphids and they agreed to help.

The next day, Ray left home slightly late, as he often did in those days, and headed for his car. A loose sock was attached by static to the back of his jacket and the tip of his tie was damp and darkened by cornflake milk. The sight of him made Tili want to gather him up in her branches. When he opened the door of his car, Ray's fingers stuck to the handle for a moment before something sticky gently relinquished its embrace. Only then did he notice the sap covering the surface of his car. He stared at the syrupy residue, and then turned and looked for the very first time at the tree under which he was parked. His eyes travelled up the solid trunk to the burgeoning canopy of greenery overhead. Tili beamed down at Ray.

After such success the lime trees decided to extend the initiative to all the cars in the road. They loved to see the people wave their fists at them in gratitude, to hear them phone the local authority and tell them all about the incredible sap. The people spent more time out on the street now, harvesting the glue from their cars with sponges and buckets, avoiding one another's eyes and staring instead with great intensity at the trees around them.

But not all the trees were content. Tili had seen something in Ray's eyes when he looked at her for the first time, and what she had seen wasn't love or gratitude, but pure, blind, animal incomprehension. When she watched him now, she could think only of the day when he and all the other people would be dead and in the ground, the UPVC sidings on their ugly houses cracked and blackened, their cheap cars rusted to dust, their brief lives as forgotten as the golden heart-shaped leaves that fell into their gardens in such numbers every year.

The Music of the Maple
Tahmima Anam

Long ago there was a misunderstanding.

The people of the ancient land of Awaaz woke up one morning to find a wall around their land. Separated from their friends on the other side, from their schools, hospitals and fields, they wept with grief. They beat their fists against the wall but it was too thick; they tried to scale the wall but it was too high. Men with guns guarded the wall and fired at anyone who dared to try and cross over.

The Citizens of the Other Side taunted the people of Awaaz. They ate their lettuce and picked their lavender. They shouted and threw clumps of earth over the wall. The people of Awaaz held the clumps to their noses, inhaling the scent of their orchards, their ancient lands.

All that remained in the possession of the people of Awaaz was a small grove of maple trees. They circled the grove and wondered what to do. Should they make firewood from the trees in anticipation of the cold months ahead? Should they clear the land and plant vegetables? The sap of these trees, they knew, was sweet. But they did not care for warmth, or food, or syrup to sweeten their mouths. What the people of Awaaz needed was a way to ease the ache around their hearts.

The wood of the maple is supple yet strong, rich, resonant, and the color of warm caramel: perfect for making music. The people of Awaaz walked around the grove and found the biggest and most majestic of the trees. They begged forgiveness of the tree as they cut it down. Then they carved a beautiful musical instrument out of the thickest part of its trunk. They stained it with beeswax until it was a rich golden brown. They called it a cello.

They built four such instruments, each a slightly different size. Then they chose their best musicians, who sat in a circle and played. The music they made sounded as if it were coming from the belly of the Earth itself. It floated over the wall and into the ears of the Citizens of the Other Side. There, the builders of walls and the pillagers of fields stopped their building and pillaging and stood still, listening. There could be no misunderstanding this music.

The musicians of Awaaz played their cellos every morning as the sun rose, and every evening as the sun set. Every day, more and more Citizens of the Other Side came to listen. They lay on the grass and sang along to the music. They held their children and warmed their backs in the sun. Instead of dirt and bricks, they began to throw flowers over the wall, and then, with gentle tosses, they passed the people of Awaaz the fruit of their orchards. Tomatoes and lettuces flew over the wall, apples and peaches and bunches of cherries.

As the sun set on the last day of the year, as the cello players of Awaaz played the final note that would see out the light, the first brick fell from the wall surrounding them.

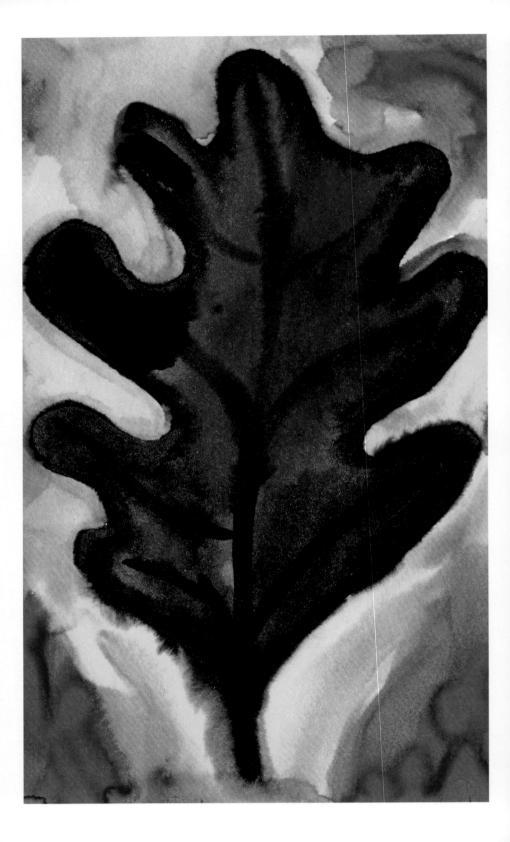

How the Oak Tree Came to Life

Maggie O'Farrell

There was once a child born to a woodcutter and his wife, a child so beautiful that the midwife, lifting him from the sodden mess of the birthing sheets, nearly dropped him. 'Saints preserve us,' she murmured, crossing herself.

The mother, raising her head from the mattress, looked at her son. 'O,' she said. A long, low sound. Her mouth a perfect, round simulacrum of the letter.

His was, you see, a beauty so surprising, so arresting that it was impossible to look away. The mind got snagged on those wide blue eyes, the long lashes, the perfect symmetry of his lips. The other mothers of the village sneaked away from their houses, from their own children, to climb the steep path to woodcutter's cottage and peer in at the windows, hoping to catch a glimpse of this astonishing child. Time and time again, the infant's mother would let the bread scorch in the stove, the milk overboil, the stew burn hard to the bottom of the pan because she was distracted by the sight of her son's face.

If anything, he grew more beautiful with each passing year. By the time he was three a mass of white-blonde curls haloed his face. His mother carried him close, passing through crowds of people who said, 'O,' and turned to see them go.

By the time he was fifteen, things came to a head. The problem was that when he walked down the main street, the girls of the village turned away from their work. They left their churning, their spinning, their baking. They put aside brooms, skillets, washing dollies, hot irons, whisks, mangles. They let slip from their hands their needles, their mops, their polishing cloths. They crowded into windows, they stoppered up doorways, they clustered at the pavement edges, just for a glimpse of his burnished curls in the breeze, the flex of his hand as he gripped the shaft of his axe, the muscled movement of his legs inside his woodcutter britches. 'O,' they sighed to each other, to him, to anyone who would listen. 'O, o, o.'

The village elders called a meeting. It wouldn't do, this kind of slipshod, female behaviour. And in the streets, too. Would it be possible, someone said, for the woodcutter's boy to wear some kind of cloak or covering, so that the womenfolk wouldn't see him as he passed by? But, someone else pointed out, how was the boy to perform his duties as a woodcutter, wearing a cloak? No, it was best all round if the womenfolk could be fitted with eye-shields, much as horses were, to prevent them from getting distracted.

The idea was an unparalleled success. The laundry was ironed. The bread was baked. The ranges were blackened and gleaming, just as before. True, the women complained about the eye-shields, said they hurt, were too tight, caused headaches. But the work got done. All was right in the village.

It just so happened that three girls who lived on the other side of the forest walked out from their village one day, with baskets to fill with blaeberries. They walked a little further into the trees than they normally did, and then a little further and further again, until they came upon a clearing. Through the hazels, the blackthorns, the red-berried rowans, they saw a boy bringing down the gleaming blade of an axe with a single, clean movement. They saw his halo of curls, the fit of his shirt, the deep water blue of his eyes. The heart-shaped leaves above him trembled and fluttered, showing their pale undersides. 'O,' the eldest girl said, bringing up a purple-stained hand to cover her open mouth. 'O,' said the middle one. 'O,' said the youngest.

The boy glanced up. He thunked his axe deep into the trunk of the lime tree and left it there for a moment while he wiped his brow with a handkerchief that the girls immediately coveted. He looked at them; they looked back at him. Then he shrugged and picked up his axe again. He was quite used to women gawping at him.

But, having never seen the boy before in their lives, the girls from the other side of the forest were even more struck by him than the women from his own village. His effect on them was ten times as strong, twenty times more devastating. They stood and stood and stood. 'O,' they said. 'O.' They stood there for a long time, well after dark and into the night, well after the woodcutter's boy had packed up his tools and gone home. So long, in fact, that their toes began to curl downwards, into the soil. They reached their arms out for him – 'Please, please' – but he did not come to them. Their arms became stuck: stretched out, scooping at empty air. Their toes, deep in the soil now, like roots, would no longer move. Their skins hardened and turned brown in the sun. And still they murmured, 'O.' Very soon in the grove of lime trees there were three new trees, the likes of which had never been seen before.

The boy's father, chancing upon them one day, circled them once, twice, three times. 'Hmm,' he said, fingering one of their strange leaves. His son said nothing.

And this is how the oak tree came to life. The noise when the wind passed through their leaves – a wistful, longing sort of sound, like a sigh, like a sob – lent itself to the name the villages gave these unusual trees: O, they called them. O trees. Which, after a while, because it was easier to say, became 'oak.'

The oak's leaves are the shape of the last thoughts that passed through the girls' heads. Wavy, curled. Massed together, in spring, and at Lammas, they look like a halo.

Red Berries
Amanda Craig

There was once a young man and his wife who lived together in a high, stony land where no trees grew. They dug a well, and built their home to stand against wind and rain, but there was one thing missing.

'We need to plant a rowan tree,' said the wife. 'The house isn't safe from evil till we do.'

Her husband scoffed at this.

'Surely you don't believe such nonsense!' he said to his wife. But he was wrong. For the rowan has many uses, both against evil and as a cure for weakness and sorrow.

As long as the year was green, the couple was as happy as two birds in one nest. Yet as the summer turned to autumn, the wife found she was expecting a child.

'I shall die if I don't have a taste of the red berries from the rowan tree,' said she. 'Though they are as bitter as gall, yet I must eat some.'

'How will I recognise the tree?' asked the husband.

'It has leaves like feathers that become gold, and white flowers that turn into red berries,' said his wife. 'If you find it, put a sprig in your jacket to ward off evil on your journey.'

But as he searched, her husband disregarded this advice. And while he was away, his wife had the baby, and named her Rowan.

Now there was a witch living nearby, and when she saw how the husband was going about, she hurried ahead to where the wife was still weak in bed.

'Let me in, and I will help you,' she said; and the wife opened the door. Then the witch smothered the poor young wife, so that she fell back like one dead. The witch threw the body of the child's true mother out on the ash-pit and took possession of the house.

When the man returned, he had eyes only for the child and never noticed that the witch had taken his wife's place. The child she treated cruelly, and would have starved her to death but for the care of the father, and for the name she had been given. So things went on, with the husband bewitched, and the child living on scraps, and the cold wind blowing all the time. Only the witch was content, for she could grow fat among them like a maggot in a bud.

One day, however, Rowan wandered out to the ash-pit, and where her tears fell a silver tree sprang up. It had feathery green leaves and a cloud of starry white flowers, and a thrush sang in its branches.

'Why are you crying?' the thrush asked.

'I cry because my mother beats me, and because I am hungry,' the child said.

'That is no mother but a witch,' said the thrush. 'Your true mother lies under this tree, with ash in her mouth and love in her heart.'

'How may I help her?' the child asked, and the thrush said, 'Water the tree every day with your tears, and talk to me as you would your mother.'

So every day from then on, the child watered the tree and talked to the thrush. In return the tree shaded her from the sun, caressing her with its leaves and showering white flowers on her face. And wherever the thrush flew, a new tree grew, with leaves that turned to gold and flowers that became red berries.

Soon the house was surrounded by a thick hedge which shut out the cold wind. The husband was glad because for the first time he could make all kinds of things he needed, from planks to handles, from spindles to cartwheels.

'Cut down the tree, husband, and burn it,' said the witch, but the man refused.

'This is indeed a most wonderful tree,' he said, and he picked a sprig of it and stuck it in his jacket. And when he had done so, he looked at the witch and asked, 'Who are you, and where is my wife?'

Then the witch was afraid, and she ran out of the house, for she knew her spell was broken. But as she passed under the rowan tree it dropped three red berries onto her head, and she fell into a little pile of ashes which the cold wind took up and blew away. Then out of the tree stepped the child's true mother, laughing and crying, and the child's father remembered her, and kissed her, and their child kissed them both. So all three of them were reunited, and could live in happiness.

Scots Pine
(A Valediction
Forbidding
Mourning)
Ali Smith

Every question holds its answer, like every answer holds its question, bound so close that they travel together like the wings on either side of a seed.

We were flying along in the car and we saw a tree off to the side. Isn't the Scots pine the loneliest tree in the world? I said. Look at it, look at that one there, standing so mournful, and apart, and dour, and elegiac. Scottish to its roots.

Uh huh, you said. If you say so.

Look at it, I said. So noble and solitary. And

it's all that remains of a huge ancient Caledonian forest. It's so romantic.

Except that as a species, you said, it also happens to be thriving all over the place, from Sutherland to Surrey, Lapland to southern Spain, Glen Affric all the way across to the forests of eastern Siberia, a Scottish-to-its-roots tree whose roots, by the way, happen to be very versatile, can develop to taproot-depth or survive on really shallow ground.

Eh, I said.

Then I didn't say anything.

Then I said: Like it's been sculpted into aloneness by the wind.

Well, aloneness, yes, you said. But that little yellow-green bird is in love with it.

What bird? I said.

Female Scottish crossbill, you said. And the male Scottish crossbill, which is redder in colour, is also in love with it. All the Scottish crossbills are. Don't be pining for the lonesome pine.

I didn't see any bird, I said.

Their crossed-over beaks are particularly good for getting the seeds out of Scots pine cones, you said.

You're making this up, I said.

No, they're real, you said, though till recently

they were so under threat that they almost stopped being real. They look like little Scottish parrots, imagine a little parrot the size of a sparrow. And without specific Scots pine cones to eat, these birds – unique to the UK, the only birds which never migrate, picky little birds whose whole diet is Scots pine cones – would be history by now.

You're looking all this up on your phone, I said.

You held your hands out in front of you in the dusk light in the car to show me there was no phone in them.

How do you know all this stuff? I said.

Same as you know all the noble solitary lonely elegiac stuff, you said, about that tree being a sign of lone buried warriors at lonely crossroads, deeply symbolic of the terrible solitariness of all things.

Well – I said.

Inhabited, you interrupted, not just by the Scottish crossbills, but by all sorts of birds from siskins all the way to eagles, and by red squirrels, by wood ants and their aphids, and by a particular kind of moth which loves pine, and many other life forms including two hundred different fungi.

I didn't know you knew any of this, I said. I didn't know you even knew there were two hundred different kinds of fungi –

Beautiful, you were saying, with the terrible pining beauty of abandonment, uh huh, and all the years of its wood being made into ships and boats, because having so much resin in it, it tends not to rot when it's wet as quickly as other wood does, and all the years of its tall straight trunk being so good for masts and pit-props and telegraph poles and fencing and being made into furniture and made into paper, and all the years of its resin d'être.

Its what? I said.

Resin, you said, the reason turpentine got made, which meant artists could clean their brushes and hands and house painters need not blame their tools; good, too, for helping violin bows glide across strings for centuries, and there's also all the years of its needles boiled and inhaled helping clear blocked chests, helping fight infection, even helping restore confidence, the Druids thought, to people who have come to dislike or disparage themselves.

Yeah, but you're not even Scottish, I said.

Your solitary lone traveller, you said, your Scots pine.

We were well past the tree now, into a treeless Highland landscape. It was already a couple of miles back, that tree. Dark was falling.

And that's how you tell what kind of tree it

is, you said. The mature trees have quite bright-coloured trunks.

Actually that's not how you tell a Scots pine, I said.

Yes it is, you said.

There's something I know about that tree that you clearly don't, I said.

There's nothing I don't know about that tree, you said.

So because I was half annoyed and half impressed, rather than say it out loud there in the car I thought it inside my head, about learning when I was small at school how you tell a Scots pine from other pines, and the way you do this is to look at the needles, because a Scots pine always grows its needles in twos together in a single sheath, never one by itself, always two, so that there are pairs of needles on every branch, countless thousands of pairs of needles on every single tree.

Come on, what? you said.

Well, how it nearly died out, I said instead. Like your birds did, the species I mean. After years of being cleared for sheep, cows, cut down and used for building.

I didn't know if this was true, but it sounded good.

But it came back, you said next to me. And it still has the ancient forest deep in its design.

I thought of the two needles, green tinged with blue, tight-bound together at one end, and I could almost smell the smell of the tree. I thought how the needles in their little sheath were like the image in a poem I only half-remembered, where two lovers are held together in the world like the points on a pair of compasses, hinged at the heart and always pushing apart.

Solitary, you said. Romantic. Alone and lonely. One tree against the world.

We drove on. Miles behind us in the landscape the tree stood evergreen in the winter and the dark and its trunk, being the trunk of a mature tree, was, yes, regardless, bright.

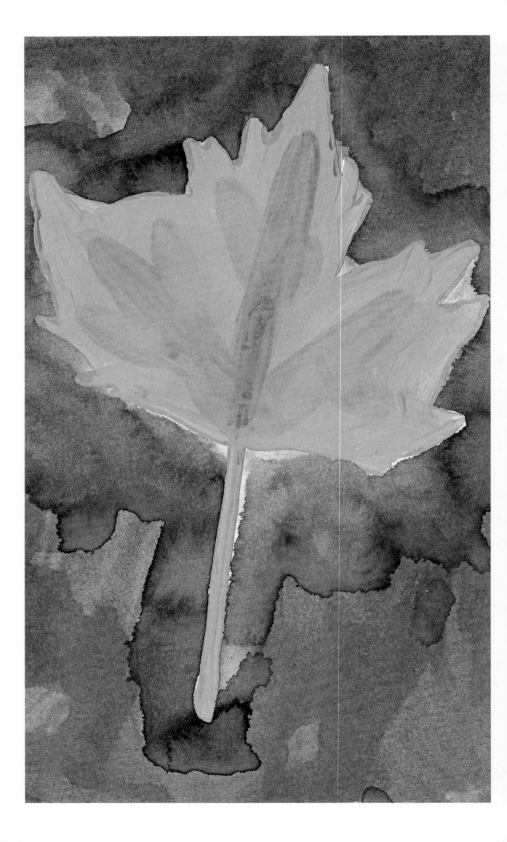

Why Sycamore Seeds Have Wings
Philip Hensher

There was once an appallingly nasty old man who had many children. 'I don't think much of that,' he would say to each of them. 'That's not what I call amounting to much in life' and 'I hope you don't think you're going out looking like that' were his favourite sentences. Although you would think, from the way he spoke to them, that he did not like his children very much, the nastiest thing he said to them was this: 'I hope you're not going to go away and leave me all on my own.'

For years, his children went nowhere when they tried to leave home. They kept on living just by their horrible old father. 'You don't have the energy to go anywhere,' he would say. 'You can't do anything for yourself. What's wrong with you?' Anyone who passed by saw the repulsive old man moaning and berating, and they would sometimes ask what was wrong. 'Sick of 'em all,' the dreadful old man would say. The passers-by would hurry away, not always hearing correctly. Because naturally nobody wants to spend time with a vile old man, full of complaints about his own children, unless they absolutely have to.

One day, the old man saw that one of his children was fashioning an apparatus of some sort. He could not quite remember what this son was called, so he said 'Hey. You. What are you up to now?' He looked more closely. About and above the son's head was a pair of broad wings, green and translucent, stretching upwards like a head-dress. Had he made them himself? What had he made them out of?

'What's that supposed to be?' the unpleasant old man said. 'Call those a pair of wings?' That was unfair, because this son had not called them anything in particular.

'I'm going to jump out of the top window of your house,' the son said. 'And my wings are going to carry me as far away from you as possible. Then I'll never have to see you again, you repulsive bully.'

'That's nice,' the horrible old idiot said. 'After everything I've done for you. But they won't work. Do you think someone like you could ever build something that would work? I've had hundreds and thousands of children over the years, and they've all been a total disappointment to me. I don't know why I ever bothered. So you needn't think that you're going to be anything other than a disappointment to me, either.'

The son nodded curtly; he shook his head; he smiled at his brothers and sisters, who had gathered together to watch; and then he looked out at the land far below, and jumped. Everyone could see that the son's flying apparatus was working first time, spinning and floating. A warm breeze lifted him, and on forest odours of pinewood and thyme and fern and warm wet earth, it carried him far away.

'O,' the brothers and sisters said in unison. Then they looked at their repellent old father, who was glaring into the forest with a curl on his upper lip and a shake of his shaggy head. 'We don't have to stay here,' one of the smallest children said to another. 'We could fly away too.'

But the nasty old man was not listening. He had never really listened to his children. 'Who do you think you are?' he shouted out into the forest after his son, the one with wings. 'Leonardo da bleeding Vinci? It'll never work, you mark my words.'

And in the forest, nobody at all heard him, and those who heard him didn't really listen.

Why Willows Weep

Salley Vickers

Long ago, when the world was still quite young, the trees and plants ruled all living things. I say 'ruled' but there was no need then for rules; rather they were the caretakers of creation as it emerged out of that obscure and uncharted place from which what is called 'creation' emerges.

The birds were the first comers into the new world, that is to say, the world after the dinosaurs were done in and done for. Except, of course, those which survived in an aerial form and reinvented themselves as birds. Having had enough of being the ruling species – for they felt, maybe rightly, that to be so was to invite hubris – the birds abdicated their position to their gracious elders, the vegetable world of trees and plants.

In time, other creatures emerged: mammoths, sabre-toothed tigers, great apes, and finally humankind lumbered into existence.

Humankind took its time, moving from a low lolloping into a rolling walk, half hands and feet, to hunch over, almost upright, making tools and weapons. It found how to make fire and began to burn wood, only the dead wood, for that burned easiest. And the trees saw to it that this new creation did no real damage. True, it liked to feed on other creatures, as well as on the fruits and seeds of the plants and trees. But it was not alone in this. The sabre-toothed tigers were also creatures of prey.

Now, the way the trees worked their benignant overseeing of the new world was through a patterning of subtle sounds that entered the spirits of the humans. One particular tree held the root and branch of this gift. If any violence was observed, beyond the ordinary necessities of living and feeding, this tree would sigh and sough and whisper so that the creatures were calmed. If any human creature wanted to kill more than it could eat, or fairly feed its family on, for instance, then this same tree let out a sigh which touched the heart of the malefactor and returned to it a sense of fellow-feeling with the other inhabitants of the world.

One day, a young female human creature was sitting by a river leaning against this tree. Across the way, she noticed a young male lifting his spear to throw at a running doe. The deer was heavily pregnant, and as the hunter raised his arm the female creature heard the sound of a great sigh very close to her ear. Behind her head, she felt the trunk of the tree shiver slightly and then begin to shake. The hunter's arm stayed poised, the spear still straight in his hand, as the deer vanished swiftly into the undergrowth. 'This is some magic,' she thought.

Drawn by what she had witnessed, the female human creature came each day to the riverside, and more and more often heard the tree expelling its strange sound. After a time, growing bolder in her fascination, she addressed the tree, 'Tell me, why do you sigh?'

Although the trees were then blessed with the means to speak, none ever did except in private to another. But surprised by this sudden question, the tree answered, 'I sigh at the sight of humankind's wrongdoings.'

'What is "wrongdoings"?' asked the young woman, who knew nothing of right or wrong.

'Harm to other living creatures,' the tree told her.

'What is "harm"?' she asked again.

'Taking what you don't need, giving pain or causing fear needlessly,' said the tree, pleased to have encountered this eager-seeming pupil.

'You sigh because you are...?'

'I sigh because I am sad,' the tree told her. 'But more than that, the sigh helps to stem the harm.'

The young woman went away and thought about this. It seemed to her a great magic and she began to want it for herself. When she next visited the tree she asked, 'Will you teach me your gift? I could help maybe to do your work and stem the harm with my sighs too.'

The woman was young and slender, with wild brown hair. She looked not unlike the tree herself and the tree thought that it might do a great good by teaching her how to sigh and to calm her own species. So it bent down and whispered the secret in her ear. At that, all the magic flew from the tree but all that entered the woman's heart was a great sorrowing at the apprehension of the harm humankind could do.

And from that time, some among humankind know right from wrong and sigh for the wrongdoings that are done. But the willow tree that lost its magic can only bend its head and weep.

Why the Yew Lives So Long
Kate Mosse

The Lives of Three Wattles, the Life of a Hound;
The Lives of Three Hounds, the Life of a Steed;
The Lives of Three Steeds, the Life of a Man;
The Lives of Three Men, the Life of an Eagle;
The Lives of Three Eagles, the Life of a Yew;
The Lives of Three Yews, the Length of an Age.

Traditional

Once, the yew tree lived and died in the company of its friends, the blackthorn and the hawthorn, the birch, the ash and the oak. The yew did not envy the blighted elm or the vulnerable hazel, with their passing brief lives, but it had no ambition to live longer than any other tree in the forest. It was content with its allotted time.

Neolithic man cleared the wildwood of Kingley Vale for grazing animals and crops, but the yew on the lower slopes did not mind. Later, Bronze Age artisans constructed burial mounds on the chalky grasslands and limestone hills above the woods, the sleeping tombs of warriors long dead. Later on the summit of Bow Hill came the Devil's Humps and Goosehill Camp and a shabby temple to Roman gods, but still the yew did not object. As time walked its steady pace on, beneath the dappled light and green shadows in the glade, Jutes and Britons and Angles breathed and lived and sighed and loved. These tribes were not the same, any more than the trees of the forest were the same. They were not fashioned by the same rituals or traditions or superstitions, yet they lived side by side, in harmonious coexistence, as did the trees. Yew with willow with pine.

But then, then.

In the year 874 came the Vikings who burned and seized and destroyed. They swept north from Chichester into the Sussex weald and the forest of Kingley Vale. The Saxon defenders sought sanctuary among the ancient green and mossy pathways where the yew trees held sway, but found no protection there. The yew could only watch and grieve as the once silent grove echoed with the violence of sword and shield, the shriek of iron and split bone. The inhumanity of it, the pointlessness of it, slipped into the leaf and the bough of the yew tree, turning the brown bark to purple. And the presentiment of death seeped into the berries, staining the pale, subtle fruit a vivid blood red.

Then the yew understood that the cycle of things had changed. Their destiny was to stand witness, memorials to those who had fallen in order that such things should not happen again. They must live until the lesson of harmony had been remembered. They did not wish it, they did not want to be left behind as the rowan and the sycamore and the beech passed into different dimensions, but they accepted it was their lot because of the battles that had been fought beneath their branches. Where each warrior fell in Kingley Vale, a yew touched the earth with its long, trailing fingers and a new tree sprang up. Soon, where the bodies of the courageous slain lay, a copse of sixty yews stood sentinel, a reminder of where the battle had been fought, and lost.

The ancient yews of Kingley Vale lived on and on, bound now to an unkind cycle of decay and rebirth and memory. Their branches grew down into the earth to form new stems. The trunks of the sixty trees rotted, but now gave life within to new trees that grew and grew until they were indistinguishable from the root.

The years passed. The generations passed, the centuries passed in the endless pattern of silver springs and shimmering summers, golden autumns and hoary winters. Still men did not learn that death breeds only death. Little by little, the reputation of the yew grew. Without wishing it, the yew became a symbol of resurrection and hope, and wisdom. In Marden and Painswick, Clifton-upon-Teme and Iona, throughout the length and breadth of the country, the yew became the favoured tree of the graveyard, of mourning, testament to the transience of memory, to the frailty of human experience.

Over eleven hundred years have passed since that first battle. If you follow the path to the centre of Kingley Vale, the sixty still stand, their branches gnarled, twisted like an old man's knuckles, their boughs weary. Tendrils trail the ground, touch the earth, paddle deep around in mossy roots. And within and above and around the wood, live green woodpeckers, red kites and buzzards, deer and stag, the chalkhill blue, holly blue and brimstone butterflies, so brief.

The people of Sussex are afraid to walk in the oldest part of the forest. They say that, at the winter solstice, the yew trees whisper to one another, singing sibilant songs of the folly of men. And so they do. Each year, if you listen carefully, you will hear the trees speak all the words they have captured in the seams of their leaves over the previous year, of the hopes, the stories, the delusions of the humans who have come to the grove to walk, to pray, to weep, to wish, to rest.

These yew trees are the oldest living things in the country. They wish it were not so. They would like to slide away, as can the ash and the oak and the elder. But human memory is brief, stupid, unconnected. Men have not yet learned to live side by side like the trees of the forest. So when the white winter dawn comes once more, and the solstice is over, the yews sigh and stretch and settle back into their ancient selves for one more year.

For the length of an age.

Contributors

Tahmima Anam is the author of *A Golden Age*, which won the 2008 Commonwealth Writers' Prize. Her second novel, *The Good Muslim*, was published in May 2011. Favourite tree: bamboo.

Rachel Billington has published twenty-two novels, of which the latest is *Glory*. She is a Vice President of English PEN and co-editor/contributor to *Inside Time*, the national newspaper for prisoners. Favourite tree: tulip.

Terence Blacker is a novelist and children's author, and writes a twice-weekly column for the *Independent*. Favourite tree: hornbeam.

Tracy Chevalier has written six novels, including the bestselling *Girl with a Pearl Earring*. Favourite tree: copper beech.

Amanda Craig is the author of six novels, which include *A Vicious Circle*, *In a Dark Wood* and most recently *Hearts and Minds*. She is the children's critic for the *Times*. Favourite tree: weeping beech.

Susan Elderkin is the author of two novels and was one of Granta's Best of Young British Novelists in 2003. Favourite tree: cedar.

William Fiennes is the bestselling author of *The Snow Geese* and *The Music Room*, and co-founder of *First Story*, which promotes writing in UK secondary schools. Favourite tree: ash.

Philippa Gregory is an historian and bestselling novelist. Favourite tree: silver birch.

Joanne Harris has written thirteen novels, including *Chocolat* and *The Lollipop Shoes*. Favourite tree: beech.

Philip Hensher has published nine novels, including *The Northern Clemency*, shortlisted for the Man Booker Prize, and the recent *King of the Badgers*. He teaches creative writing at the University of Exeter, and is a book reviewer and columnist. In 2003 he was one of Granta's Best of Young British Novelists. Favourite tree: cherry.

Richard Mabey's books include *Nature Cure*, *Weeds* and the prize-winning *Flora Britannica*. He is Patron of the John Clare Society. Favourite tree: beech.

Maria McCann is the author of *As Meat Loves Salt* and *The Wilding*. Favourite tree: elder.

Blake Morrison has written poetry, fiction and memoir. His latest novel is *The Last Weekend*. Favourite tree: horse chestnut.

Kate Mosse is the author of two non-fiction books, seven novels – including the international bestselling *Labyrinth* – and two plays. Favourite tree: cedar.

Maggie O'Farrell is the author of seven novels, including *The Hand That First Held Mine*. She lives in Edinburgh, among many trees. Favourite tree: gingko.

Catherine O'Flynn has written three novels, including *The News Where You Are* and *What Was Lost*, which won the Costa First Novel Award. Favourite tree: cherry.

James Robertson is a poet and author of five novels, including *The Testament of Gideon Mack* and *And the Land Lay Still*. Favourite tree: Scots pine.

Leanne Shapton is the author of *Important Artifacts and Personal Property from the Collection of Harold Morris and Lenore Doolan, Including Books, Street Fashion and Jewelry*. Her most recent book is *The Native Trees of Canada*. Favourite tree: Manitoba maple.

Ali Smith is the author of eight novels, including *There But For The*, and has won or been nominated for the Man Booker, the Orange Prize and the Whitbread Novel of the Year. Favourite tree: all of them.

Salley Vickers is the author of eight novels, including the bestselling *Miss Garnet's Angel*, and a short story collection. Favourite tree: She is named 'Salley' after William Butler Yeats's poem, 'Down by the salley gardens,' which in Irish means willow. So her favourite tree might be willow but in fact is the rowan.

The Woodland Trust

Established for almost four decades and committed to the welfare of woods and trees, the Woodland Trust is the UK's leading woodland conservation charity.

Our vision is for a UK rich in woods and trees that can be enjoyed and valued by everyone.

One of the least wooded countries in Europe, the UK has seen its woodland heritage spiral downwards in the last 80 years, as almost half our irreplaceable ancient woodland has been damaged or lost. This priceless resource is at least 400 years old and provides a diverse and inimitable home to more animals, plants, insects and birds than any other habitat in the UK. It is no exaggeration to call it our equivalent of the rainforest.

We believe all remaining ancient woodland should be protected, and buffered with new trees to act as a shield from future harm. And to counteract the damage done in previous decades we want to double native woodland cover by 2050, bringing together millions of people, landowners, organisations and communities across the UK to plant trees.

That's why we're so grateful to the authors of this collection, who have shared their love of woodland to inspire others to create, cherish and take care of it too.

Trees purify the air and cleanse the soil, form a natural defence against flooding, provide shelter from the elements and offer a sustainable supply of eco-friendly fuel. Home to a vast array of wildlife, they create places where children can play, adults reflect, birds and plant life flourish and communities come together.

You can help us achieve our vision by becoming a member, donating, or planting trees. To get involved please call 0800 026 9650 or visit woodlandtrust.org.uk

IndieBooks is an artisan publisher committed
to producing books to the highest possible
editorial and production standards while
remaining affordable for a wide audience.
You can buy our titles direct at
indiebooks.co.uk
or from all good bookshops.